It is Often Said

Often

Said

Tim Hegg

"The Law is not Spiritual"

"Yeshua's Law Replaced the Law of Moses"

"We Have the Spirit ...Who Needs the Letter?"

Comments and Comparisons of Traditional
Christian Theology and Hebraic Thought  Volume 2

It is Often Said

Tim Hegg

"The Law is not Spiritual"

"Yeshua's Law Replaced the Law of Moses"

"We Have the Spirit ...Who Needs the Letter?"

FIRST FRUITS OF
ZION

Proclaiming the Torah and its way
of life, fully centered on Messiah,
to today's People of God

From a series of articles
first published in
messiah magazine

Second Edition, January 2006

Printed in the United States of America

Catalog Information: Theology
CBA Category Information: BST, DOT, OTT
ISBN 1-892124-05-X

Unless otherwise indicated, Scripture quotations in this publication are from the NEW AMERICAN STANDARD BIBLE®, Copyright © 1960, 1962, 1963, 1968, 1971, 1972, 1973, 1975, 1977, 1995 by The Lockman Foundation. Used by permission. Throughout this publication the word *Christ* is rendered "Messiah", *Jesus* is rendered "Yeshua" and *Law* is rendered "Torah". *(www.Lockman.org)*

Design: Avner Wolff

First Fruits of Zion

PO Box 620099
Littleton, Colorado 80162–0099 USA
Phone (303) 933–2119 or (800) 775–4807
Fax (303) 933–0997
www.ffoz.org

Additional Study Resources
Torah Club, a monthly Torah Study Course
HaYesod, a fourteen-week Hebraic Study Course
messiah magazine

Other Books by Tim Hegg
The Letter Writer
ISBN 1-892124-16-5
Fellowheirs
ISBN 1-892124-06-8

For additional information, please visit http://www.ffoz.org

Contents

Foreword

Shalom! Thank you for purchasing *It is Often Said, Volume 2*. This is a continuation of the series of articles that first appeared in *messiah magazine*, written by my friend and colleague Tim Hegg. I pray this booklet will be a useful resource for you in your studies.

A generation after the passing of Saul of Tarsus, there lived a highly influential church leader named Marcion (ca. 130 CE). In his book *Paul the Jewish Theologian*, Brad Young writes, "On the one hand, early church leaders condemned Marcion as a heretic (144 CE), but on the other, they were influenced by his theological reflection. Even today Marcion-like ideas continue to circulate, exerting influence in Christian teachings" (pp. 33–34). One of these impressionable ideas was calling the Hebrew Bible (*Tanakh*) "The Old Testament," indicating that the contents of that book no longer have application for all those who believe in Yeshua.

Bible teachers who have unwittingly expounded Marcion's thoughts have influenced believers in greater ways than we may think. In this volume we will continue to tackle the issues that separate the Torah from the "New Testament" and divide the Lord's complete revelation into separate parts. We support the position that Torah is a valid expression of a life of belief in the God of Abraham, Isaac and Jacob.

Our mission at First Fruits of Zion is to publish professional, high-quality resources that teach the validity of a Torah-centered lifestyle. FFOZ's teachings are ultimately a stepping-stone toward the application of these truths within a community context, which will lead people into a brand-new way of life, one of a holy and pure lifestyle devoted to God. The living out of God's Torah does not gain us merit or right standing before God. Rather it allows God's nature and character to be revealed through His sanctified people.

Through these teachings we pray that many will recognize the need to return to a moral and ethical life as defined by the whole of Scripture which results in a pure declaration of the life that can only be found in God.

We are continually publishing new resources for the study of the Hebraic roots of the Christian faith. We also produce Messiah-centric, Torah-based studies called Torah Club. Each volume covers weekly Torah readings in the annual cycle of the Jewish calendar. For more information call 1–800–775–4807, or visit our website at www.ffoz.org.

Boaz Michael
FOUNDER, FIRST FRUITS OF ZION
WWW.FFOZ.ORG

Preface

The words *letter* and *Spirit* have been regularly interpreted as referring to the "Old Testament" (*Tanakh*) or the "Law" in contrast to the "New Testament" (Apostolic Scriptures) ministry of the Spirit of God. Since Paul writes that "the letter kills but the Spirit gives life," (2 Corinthians 3:6) it is taught that the Torah and the Spirit are in opposition and that therefore the way of the Spirit is not the way of Torah.

But what exactly does Paul mean when he makes a contrast between the terms *letter* and *Spirit*? Is Paul saying that we no longer need the direction of the *Tanakh* (the only Scriptures that existed in Paul's day), or is he saying something else that we have misunderstood? In this second volume of *It is Often Said*, we will be answering these questions.

As the centuries have passed, our distance from the historical and contextual setting of the Scriptures has increased. We are generally ignorant of what was going on in the generations in which the biblical texts were written. Idioms and literary expressions that are used in the Apostolic Scriptures, if misunderstood or passed over, will inevitably yield wrong interpretations. The Apostle Peter was correct when talking about the writings of Paul when he said, "Some things [are] hard to understand, which the untaught and unstable distort" (2 Peter 3:16).

Nowhere is this more evident than in today's confusion about God's Torah. The popular teachings are that: 1) The Law is done away with; 2) The principles of the "Old Testament" are good for us because they form the foundation for many of the "New Testament" teachings, but we aren't supposed to literally obey them; 3) The moral aspects of the Law are extracted and considered worthy, but the remainder is considered relevant only for bygone eras.

This confusion causes division between the multitude of denominations and believers of different faiths. What happened to "One Lord, one faith, one baptism" (Ephesians 4:5)?

How can we all stand together when we can't even agree about the nature and purpose of the authority of Scripture?

Could it be that we are so far off the mark because we have forced our individual doctrines and creeds upon the Scriptures instead of letting the Scriptures speak for themselves? Is it possible that we are so confused regarding the authority and unity of Scripture that we cannot discern the simple truth that our God does "not change" (Malachi 3:6)?

Open your mind and heart to the following pages and allow the Scriptures to speak for themselves. Follow the counsel of the prophet Isaiah and compare all that you know "To the Torah and to the testimony! If they do not speak according to this word, it is because they have no dawn" (Isaiah 8:20).

We must challenge ourselves to find consistency in the teachings of the Bible from Genesis through Revelation. We need to apply this common, basic understanding of Scripture in a literal way, dispelling thousands of years of Torah neglect and misunderstanding. We hope that the body of Messiah will be brought together on the firm foundation of the authority of the Word of God.

It is imperative that we embrace with a full heart what has been given by our Creator—His revelation to us—His Scriptures.

As you read through this book you will find yourself coming across terminology you may not be familiar with. We are using the original Hebrew translation for many commonly used words because the Hebrew word gives a much fuller meaning. Yeshua is Jesus' Hebrew name. His name means "salvation." The meaning of His name alone is good reason to use it. We also use the word *Torah* when referring to the first five books of the Bible. This word means "teaching or instruction" in the Hebrew. This is a much more accurate definition of the books of Moses than the more commonly used term *law*. The word *Tanakh* is used in place of Old Testament. *Tanakh* is an acronym formed from the three sections of the Hebrew Bible—the *Torah*, the *Nevi'im* (Prophets), and the *Ketuvim* (Writings).

Rather than calling His disciples to some new level of spirituality, Yeshua is exhorting His followers to recover the inspired meaning of God's revelation in the Torah. In a radical way He cuts through the tangle of man-made laws to uncover the spiritual wealth of God's Torah. He calls us to listen to the whole symphony and appreciate its masterful unity.

It is Often Said

"The Law is not Spiritual"

In our modern world, religion has sought its own way. Like water that flows where the topography allows, man has fashioned his religion to follow the contours of his own desires. Rather than consider the revelation of God in the Bible as the inspired symphony of the eternal Creator, we have viewed the Bible more along the lines of the "Top 40." From one era to another, this part or that part makes it to the top of the charts while the rest is discarded as the music of a bygone era.

But we are coming to realize that the Word of God is one song—one melody sung throughout the ages, calling us to worship our Creator. And Yeshua is the theme of that symphony. We hear variations on this theme from the Torah, the Prophets, the Writings, and the Apostles, but we recognize each movement as an integral part of the whole.

In Volume One of *It is Often Said*, we looked at the meaning of Yeshua's words when He declared that He had come to "fulfill the Torah and the Prophets." When considered within the context of Matthew 5, where this statement is found, we saw that by "fulfill" He meant "confirm" or "establish," and thus His intention to teach His disciples the proper interpretation of Torah as well as its correct implementation within their lives.

Traditionally the verses that follow are interpreted to mean that He was replacing the teaching of Torah with His own teaching. "You have heard it said ... but I say to you ..." appears at first reading to indicate just that. But, as previously noted, this contrast between what has been "heard" and what Yeshua was "saying" was a technique used by teachers of His day to contrast a well-known interpretation with their own unique emphasis. In using such language, Yeshua was not negating Torah but calling His disciples back to a proper interpretation of it, an interpretation unshackled from the traditions that had often clouded the meaning and proper application of the sacred text.

Part of what fuels the traditional interpretation (that Yeshua's teaching replaces the Torah) is the mistaken notion that believers after the time of Yeshua have a greater spirituality than believers before His coming. This is usually based on the belief that the Spirit became active in believers only after the time of Yeshua.

Therefore, before we can investigate the words of Yeshua in Matthew 5–7, we must first consider this claim of greater spirituality.

The Claim of Greater Spirituality

Are believers today more spiritual than the believers who lived before Yeshua? The reason this question arises in discussions of Torah-life is obvious. If we have arrived at a time when the work of the Spirit within individuals exists, and therefore when believers have a greater measure of spirituality than those in ancient Israel, we have also arrived at a time when the teachings of Yeshua and the Apostles have bypassed Torah and made it obsolete. Subsequently, the conclusion many people hold is also obvious. They often say, "Any acceptance of the Torah's relevance for today would be like renouncing the greater level of spirituality we now possess and settling for the inferior spirituality of the old covenant." It is understandable, therefore, how reading "You have heard it said ... but I say to you ..." could fuel such a conclusion. Yeshua's words would be read as meaning "Leave the Torah behind and move forward to the greater spirituality gained by My teaching."

This viewpoint is usually based upon a number of arguments, but perhaps those most often encountered are:

- ☞ First, that Yeshua's teaching speaks to the heart, while the Torah is primarily concerned with externals.

- ☞ Second, that the Torah speaks from an "old covenant" viewpoint, while Yeshua teaches the "new covenant."

- ☞ Third, that the Spirit was not active before the coming of Yeshua, at least within individuals. Therefore, we should not expect a high level of spirituality during the era of the "Old Testament."

Let's examine each of these arguments carefully.

"Yeshua speaks to the heart" vs. "The Torah is concerned about externals."

If one is willing to read the Scriptures without prejudice, it becomes clear that this contrast between internal versus external is a fabrication. Yeshua instructed His disciples to pay attention to even the smallest stroke of the Torah (Matthew 5:18), and this surely must include what the Torah commands regarding one's outward actions. In fact, Yeshua clearly teaches that one's "fruit" (actions) is what proves one's heart condition (Matthew 7:17–19). He never considers one's "spirituality" to be internal. For if one is truly spiritual, this will be known by his life of obedience. One who claims to be spiritual but does not obey God is self-deceived. A tree that does not bear fruit is cut down and cast into the fire.

The Torah teaches the same message. The commandments must first be written on the heart before they can govern one's life (Deuteronomy 6:6; 11:18; cf. Proverbs 4:23). This is why the Torah demands that one's heart be circumcised (Deuteronomy 10:16; 30:6). Israel's disobedience is attributed to a "heart of stone" (Ezekiel 11:19).

The Apostles teach this same lesson. James finds no place for mere confession without accompanying righteous deeds (James 2:14–18), and Paul exhorts us that it is not one who hears the Torah, but one who actually does it that is justified (Romans 2:13). The consistent message of the Scriptures, cover to cover, is that when God changes the heart, one's actions change as well.

Often the idea of loving God is construed as an inward attitude, a matter of the heart. And surely loving God involves the submission of one's soul to Him. But it is instructive to note how often the idea of "loving God" is paired with "keeping His commandments" (Exodus 20:6; Deuteronomy 5:10; 7:9; 11:1, 13; 30:16; Joshua 22:5; Nehemiah 1:5; Daniel 9:4). Yeshua makes the same claim regarding those who love Him (John 14:15, 21).

Yes, Yeshua speaks to the heart in His teaching, but in doing so He is calling the people back to listen to the Torah's message which was also directed to the heart. Yeshua is not writing a new song—He and Moses sing the same melody.

"The Torah is old covenant" vs. "Yeshua teaches the new covenant."

The first issue that should be addressed is the misunderstanding of the labels "old covenant" and "new covenant." Contrary to the popular use of these terms, they do not describe dispensations or periods of time. While the normal understanding is that the old covenant describes the life of God's people before the coming of Yeshua, and the new covenant describes their life after the coming of Yeshua, no such definition can be found in the Scriptures.

Then what do the labels "old covenant" and "new covenant" mean? The new covenant describes the final salvation of the

It is common in our day to hear people express their thinking that the Spirit of God began His work within individual believers only after the coming of Messiah.

～・～

nation of Israel when, through faith, her sins will be forgiven and the Torah will be written on her heart (Jeremiah 31:31–34). For the first time in earth's history, Israel as a whole will be fully submitted to God and His Messiah. Then she will have the Torah written on her heart, and she will walk in His ways. And while all who are true believers form a kind of "first fruits" of the new covenant, its fulfillment awaits the final ingathering of Israel and her last days' revival in faith.

The old covenant (used only one time in the Bible, 2 Corinthians 3:14) is an expression used only by Paul to describe a person who reads the *Tanakh* apart from the illuminating work of the Spirit. When this occurs, the reader does not see Yeshua in the *Tanakh* because a veil lies over his heart. As long as he reads the *Tanakh* as mere letters without the illuminating work of the Spirit he will never see the Messiah of whom the Prophets spoke (2 Corinthians 3:16ff). But when these same Scriptures—the Torah, the Prophets, and the Writings, the three types of writings in the *Tanakh*—are read with the veil removed by the Spirit, these same words reveal Messiah and bring the reader to saving faith. Without the Spirit the *Tanakh* is the "old covenant," but with the Spirit the *Tanakh* leads to Messiah and the Torah is written on the heart, fulfilling the promise of the "new covenant."

The writers of Scripture did not define "old" and "new" covenants as successive eras or generations, the old covenant being "back then" and the new covenant being "now." Furthermore, for Paul, the "old covenant" is understood to mean that one has no true knowledge of Yeshua as the Messiah. When the Scriptures are read without the illumination of the Spirit, Yeshua is veiled, and that is what Paul calls the "old covenant." Therefore, for Paul, no one reading the Scriptures as an old covenant could be saved.

Though the misunderstanding of "old covenant" vs. "new covenant" has been the standard filter through which the Scriptures have been read in our times, we must be willing to let the sacred text speak on its own. If we do, we will find no reason to think that Yeshua opposed Moses as though He were replacing the old covenant with the new covenant.

"The Spirit's work began after the coming of Yeshua."

It is common in our day to hear people express their thinking that the Spirit of God began His work within individual believers only after the coming of Messiah. Since the Spirit was poured out on Pentecost following the ascension of Yeshua, it is presumed that He was inactive prior to that time. This popular belief acknowledges that the Spirit worked within some individuals in ancient Israel (such as prophets, kings, and artisans) but that normally He did not indwell the believer, nor did He assist him in sanctification.

When one stops to contemplate this point of view, its inadequacies are immediately seen. The most obvious objection to be raised is that it necessitates two ways of salvation. Salvation is never presented in Scripture as merely the forgiveness of sin. The goal of salvation is holiness: "Be holy, for I … am holy." (Leviticus 19:2, cf. 1 Peter 1:15) God's salvation is not a "fire escape" for sinners, but a divine work whereby He creates a people fit for His dwelling. The goal of salvation is that God should dwell among His people. If God requires holiness as the prerequisite for His dwelling, the Spirit must be active in bringing about this holiness.

Indeed, the whole scope of salvation, from justification through sanctification, is described by the Apostles as involving the work of the Spirit of God. Paul uses Abraham and David

(Romans 4) as the models for salvation by faith. He believed they were saved the same way he was, through the Spirit. Look at how Paul describes the Spirit's part in the work of salvation:

- Circumcision of the heart is accomplished by the Spirit (Romans 2:29), and the Torah exhorted the people of Moses' day to have their hearts circumcised (cf. Deuteronomy 10:16; 30:6). Jeremiah exhorted the people to the same action (Jeremiah 4:4).

- Apart from the Spirit, Yeshua is veiled in the Torah (2 Corinthians 3). If those redeemed in ancient times where saved as we are (i.e., by faith in Yeshua), they did so only as the Spirit unveiled Him in the *Tanakh*, opened their eyes to see Him, and gave them faith to believe.

- Apart from the Spirit, the Torah only brings condemnation, damnation, and death (2 Corinthians 3; Romans 8:2; Romans 8:9ff). How then could David write that the Torah restores the soul unless the Spirit was active in this restoration (Psalm 19:7ff)?

- The requirements of the Torah can only be lived out by those who have the Spirit (Romans 8:9ff). Those who do not have the Spirit cannot submit to the Torah. Since it is clear that those who were of true faith in ancient Israel did submit to the Torah, we must conclude they had the Spirit.

- The deeds of the flesh can only be put to death by the Spirit (Romans 8:13). Did the believers in ancient Israel put to death the deeds of the flesh? If not, how could they have obtained any personal holiness?

- Knowledge that one is truly a child of God is given by the Spirit (Romans 8:16). Did the believers of old know they were God's children? Surely they did, for they are put forward as models of holiness for us to follow (Noah, 2 Peter 2:4; Elijah, James 5:17; Abraham, Romans 4:16, 19; Sarah, 1 Peter 3:6; and all those listed in Hebrews 11).

- The Spirit helps us in our prayers, taking our requests before God (Romans 8:26). Were the believers of old helped in their prayers? If not, were their prayers effective? By all accounts they were. (Note the prayer of Elijah in James 5:17.) This presupposes the presence of the Spirit aiding them in their prayers.

- No one can know the thoughts of God apart from the Spirit's work of revelation/illumination (1 Corinthians 2:10ff). Did the believers of old know the thoughts of God? Surely they did, as attested throughout the *Tanakh.*

- Sanctification is the work of the Spirit of God (1 Corinthians 6:11), and it is only in the Spirit that one is able to overcome the flesh (Galatians 5:16). Were the believers of old being sanctified? Were they able to overcome the flesh?

- Eternal life is connected with the righteousness produced by the Spirit (Galatians 6:8). Did the believers of old possess eternal life?

- Salvation is possible only through the washing of regeneration and the renewing of the Holy

Spirit (Titus 3:5). Did the believers of old
possess salvation?

The only conclusion that can be reached, based upon the
teaching of the Apostles themselves, is that the Holy Spirit was
active in the salvation of ancient Israelites even as He is active
now. This work of the Spirit in regeneration (new birth) and
sanctification (holiness) is therefore as much a part of salvation before Yeshua as after Him. Granted, the special work of
the Spirit for the ingathering of the nations was something the
prophets anticipated, and it was manifested in His outpouring
at Pentecost following Yeshua's ascension. But the basic work
of salvation has always been the engagement of God's Spirit, in
all who are saved, in every generation.

Therefore, any hermeneutical presupposition that begins
with the notion that Yeshua was teaching a different way of
holiness must be rejected at the outset. If we are to understand
Yeshua's teaching in the Sermon on the Mount, we must begin
with the premise that God's way of salvation as taught in the
Torah is precisely the same salvation accomplished by Yeshua
and proclaimed by His Apostles.

It is with this background in mind that we must read Yeshua's
words in Matthew 5:21–43. Rather than calling His disciples to
some new level of spirituality, Yeshua is exhorting His followers
to recover the inspired meaning of God's revelation in the Torah.
In a radical way He cuts through the tangle of man-made laws to
uncover the spiritual wealth of God's Torah. He calls us to listen
to the whole symphony and appreciate its masterful unity.

Light and Weighty Laws

The evaluation of the commandments was a significant topic in
early Judaism if the subsequent literature (*Mishnah, Midrashim,
Talmud*) is any indication. As Urbach shows, there were various
viewpoints among the sages.

The question of the relative value of the commandments found expression in many varied forms in
the teaching of the Sages. On the one hand we find
dicta that proclaim the absolute equality of all the
precepts, and on the other we encounter clear dis-
tinctions drawn between more important and less
important commandments, and methods of clas-
sifying precepts and transgressions according to
various criteria.[1]

Various sages and schools gave different criteria of evaluation for the commandments. For instance, Rav Judah comments
on m.*Shevuot* 1.6, saying:

This is the meaning ... the light [transgressions] are
those involving positive or negative commandments;
and the grave [transgressions] are those punished by
"extinction" or death by sentence of the court.[2]

He based the criteria for valuation of the commandments
on the severity of the penalty for their transgression.

R. ben Azzai saw it differently. On the verse "Only be stead-
fast in not eating the blood," he remarked:

Now there are three hundred similar positive precepts in the Torah! It comes to teach us, therefore,
that if in regard to blood, than which there is no
lighter precept among all the commandments,
Scripture admonished you thus, how much more so
in the case of the other precepts.[3]

Urbach explains:

The eating of the blood is something repulsive; conse-
quently it is easy to abstain from it. Lightness and
stringency are not measured by the extent of the
reward or punishment involved in doing the precept or transgression, but according to the effort

To live life with the notion that one can neglect the "lighter" laws and not fall prey to breaking the "weightier" ones is misguided.

⟡

required to fulfill the commandments or to refrain from the transgressions. So, too, a precept not entailing expenditure of money, or involving danger to life, is called "a light commandment".[4]

Yeshua also came to a conclusion on laws that were light[5] and those that were heavy. He was in agreement with those who proclaimed a law such as honoring father and mother an extremely stringent or heavy one, for it is on this very basis that He rebukes the Pharisee. He admonishes them not to neglect the "weightier" matters of the Torah by becoming entangled in the lighter precepts: "But these are the things you should have done without neglecting the others" (Matthew 23:23). Yeshua was fully aware of, and a participant in, the debate over the valuation of commandments. In the end, however, the majority agreed with Yeshua's position, as we read in *Avot*:

> And be heedful of a light precept as of a weighty one, for you know not the reward given for the precepts.[6]

It was not only Yeshua who saw main-stream Pharisaism in need of rebuke. The Qumran society had also taken a stand against them in regard to the valuation of commandments. 4QPsa 1:27 it states that the Pharisees "have chosen the light matters." By this we might understand that they had chosen those commandments that required the least sacrifice on their part—those that could be performed without a humbling of the soul, and especially those that could be seen publicly.

With this before us, then, it is possible to interpret Yeshua's teaching as addressing the issue of commandment evaluation. Some Pharisees had chosen to do the "light" commandments, those that required the least amount of effort to fulfill (though had plenty of public notice). Yet they were constantly neglecting (and thus breaking) the weightier ones, those that required a greater sacrifice to fulfill (and were often not public).

In stating at the opening that each and every commandment (regardless of its valuation) was important, Yeshua sets the stage for His antitheses. But He does it in a most intriguing way. He states a law that all would agree was valued as weighty (introduced by "You have heard it said"), then shows that the inward heart attitude is just as weighty a commandment (introduced by "but I say to you"). What He teaches is this: While there are commandments designated light and those designated heavy, all the precepts of God are important and must be carried out from the heart. To live life with the notion that one can neglect the "lighter" laws and not fall prey to breaking the "weightier" ones is misguided.

Finally

Our Savior's teaching in what has been called the Sermon on the Mount reinforces the eternal value of the Torah which He came to establish, not abolish. The Torah will be established in the lives of His disciples when its message is written on the heart and lived out accordingly. Far from teaching a new or innovative spirituality, Yeshua unwraps the Torah from man-made restrictions, allowing its theme to resonate throughout the rest of God's inspired Scriptures. Like a symphony that introduces the theme in its opening movement, the Torah introduces God's theme, one that sings of the beauty of Messiah. It was this Torah melody Yeshua was singing.

"The Law is not Spiritual"

"Yeshua replaced the 'Old Testament' law with a
new spirituality. The old law was harsh and only
concerned with externals, while He preached
a new message of love and spirituality."

Yes, Yeshua speaks to the heart in His teaching, but in doing so He is calling the people back to listen to the Torah's message which was also directed to the heart (Exodus 20:6; Deuteronomy 5:10; 7:9; 11:1, 13; 30:16). Yeshua is not writing a new song—He and Moses sing the same melody.

"The Law was temporary! Since it was only a
burden on the necks of God's people, they looked
forward to the time when the Messiah would come
and replace it with His new, eternal truths."

The writers of Scripture did not define "old" and "new" covenants as successive eras or generations, the old covenant being "back then" and the new covenant being "now." For Paul the "old covenant" is understood to mean that one has no true knowledge of Yeshua as the Messiah. When the Scriptures are read without the illumination of the Spirit, Yeshua is veiled, and that is what Paul calls the "old covenant." Therefore, no one under the old covenant could be saved.

> "The reason people in ancient Israel could never experience a true, spiritual relationship with God is because they did not have the Spirit of God. Only believers after the coming of Yeshua were indwelt with the Spirit."

The Holy Spirit was active in the salvation of the ancient Israelites even as He is active now. This work of the Spirit in regeneration (new birth) and sanctification (holiness) is therefore as much a part of salvation before Yeshua as after Him. Granted, the special work of the Spirit for the ingathering of the nations was something the prophets anticipated, and was manifested in His outpouring at Pentecost following Yeshua's ascension. But the basic work of salvation has always been the engagement of God's Spirit, in all who are saved, in every generation.

Study Questions

~~~~~~~~~~~~

"The Law is not Spiritual"

1. How would you respond to someone who says the Torah is only concerned with externals? (Consider verses like Deuteronomy 6:6; 8:2; 10:12–21). If Yeshua teaches us to obey Torah (Matthew 5:17–20; 28:19-20), what does this indicate about His view of the Torah?

2. Discuss the meaning of "new covenant" and "old covenant" (Jeremiah 31:31–34; 2 Corinthians 3:14). With whom is the new covenant made? What does God do with the Torah in the new covenant? What is veiled in the old covenant?

3. Are there two ways of salvation, one for the people who lived before Yeshua, and another for those who lived after He came? If not, what does this say about the place of Torah in God's plan of salvation?

4. How did Yeshua evaluate the commandments under the general heading of "light" and "weighty"? Does He teach that it is acceptable to neglect the "light" commandments and concentrate only on the "weighty" ones? What are the implications of this for our lives today?

5. Mark 12:29–33 teaches us that loving God and our neighbor is more valuable than all burnt offerings and sacrifices. Is this something new or did the Torah also teach this? (Consider Leviticus 19:2; Deuteronomy 10:16; Ezekiel 11:19–20; Hosea 6:6; Proverbs 21:3.) What does this imply about the continuity of God's revelation in the Scriptures? A living copy of the Torah is being written on our hearts. This inner Torah does not negate the written Torah. Instead it is supposed to become a moral reflex for us that enables us to walk in genuine obedience. To the extent that we do so, we are living lives like Messiah, Who was the perfect revelation of godliness in human form. (See Jeremiah 31:33; John 15:10.)

Far from abandoning the Torah, or relegating it to an inferior status, Yeshua called the people of His day, and us in our day, to embrace the Torah as God's gracious revelation of His own holiness and His instruction for our own righteous living. This Torah was given not to build men's kingdoms, but God's own kingdom of righteousness.

It is Often Said

"Yeshua's Law Replaced the Law of Moses"

Traditionally the Sermon on the Mount has become the basis for the often-heard statements about the inferior nature of the Torah when compared with the teachings of Yeshua. "You have heard it said ... but I say to you" is usually interpreted to mean that Yeshua contrasted His teaching with the teaching of the Torah, and that He actually replaced the Torah with His instructions. However, I suggested previously that such an interpretation was a misreading of the Matthew text. Historically, rabbis would indicate the common understanding of a text with the introductory "You have heard ...." and then contrast it with their own interpretation, introduced by "but I say to you." This was what Yeshua was doing as well. Clearly, to offer a different interpretation is far different from negating the Torah altogether!

Furthermore, Yeshua's interpretation of the Torah was one that encouraged His listeners to return to its simple, straightforward application, one that flowed from a genuine desire to please God, not man. In doing so, He often went cross-grain to the complicated teachings of His day and therefore raised the ire of the established sages whose efforts at building fences around the Torah had rendered it mired in a sea of red tape. It is in this context that we hear His words "You have heard it said … but I say to you …" Far from dismissing the Torah, Yeshua was calling the people back to its holy message, one that called the people of Israel and all those who would join her into a covenant relationship with the Creator.

Consider, as we look at each section, how Yeshua is calling us back to listen to the Torah as God originally gave it.

Hatred and Murder (Matthew 5:21ff)

Yeshua begins with an obvious case: hatred that leads to murder. Everyone knew the story of Joseph and his brothers. Three times in the opening narrative (Genesis 37:4, 5, 8) Joseph's brothers are said to hate him. And where does this lead? They were willing to murder him. So murder, which was classed by some as a weighty commandment (since it drew the death penalty) is linked to hatred (considered a light commandment). Yeshua, however, wishes to draw attention to the weighty matter of hatred, for if left unchecked, it leads to murder.

This is referred to in *Sifre* Deuteronomy 19:11

> If any man hates his neighbor, and lies in wait for him, and attacks him [and wounds him mortally so that he dies …] (Deuteronomy 19:11). From there it was deduced: if a man has transgressed a light commandment, he will finally transgress a weighty commandment. If he transgress [the commandment]: "You shall love your neighbor as yourself" (Lev 19:18), he will finally transgress [the commandment] "You shall not take vengeance or bear any grudge" (ibid.), and the [commandment] "You shall not hate your brother" (Lev 19:17), and the [commandment] "that your brother may live beside you" (Lev 25:36)—until he will (finally) be led to bloodshed. Therefore it is

said: "If any man hates his neighbor and lies in wait for him and attacks him."[7]

The Torah itself teaches this. We are commanded to do good to those who hates us:

> If you see the donkey of one who hates you lying helpless under its load, you shall refrain from leaving it to him, you shall surely release it with him. (Exodus 23:5)

> You shall not hate your fellow countryman in your heart; you may surely reprove your neighbor, but shall not incur sin because of him. (Leviticus 19:17)

Yeshua calls His disciples to consider the important and weighty task of guarding the heart as the loving expression of one who intends to please the Father. If a capital offense like murder begins in the heart, one is wise to consider hatred as the first step toward murder. This radical approach to holiness is what Yeshua requires of His disciples because it is what the Torah has always taught.

Adultery and Divorce (Matthew 5:27ff)

The words of Yeshua regarding adultery "contain nothing new or off the Rabbinic line."[8] Adultery is forbidden "both with the eye and in the heart."[9] Resh Lakish, alluding to Job 24:15, said, "The verse is intended to indicate that one can commit adultery with the eye as well as with the body."[10]

In a Talmudic story, a man had an illegitimate longing for a certain woman. The doctor said he could not be cured unless his desire was gratified, at least partially. However, the sages said, "Then let him die. Evil thoughts (i.e., lustful thoughts) are even worse than lustful deeds."[11]

The high number of divorces in Yeshua's day betrayed a practice different from the sages' ideology. The houses of Hillel and Shammai had argued about what constituted legitimate

> When the Torah is unveiled to reveal the Living Torah, Yeshua, it functions as the divinely inspired foundation for the individual, the family, and the community.

～～

divorce, based upon the interpretation of, *ervat davar*, "an indecent thing" in Deuteronomy 24:1. But in their debates they had neglected to emphasize the reason divorce was wrong in the first place: it disregarded the intentions of God that the husband and wife should be one (Genesis 2:24). Seeking only to know when divorce was legal, the sages had de-emphasized the sanctity of marriage and unwittingly opened the door for men to let sexual lust go unchecked.

So rampant was the problem of divorce that some sages attempted to diminish its legitimacy, for they saw that its abuse was devastating. In commenting on Malachi 2:16–17, R. Eleazar taught that "the very altar drops tears on every one who divorces the wife of his youth."[12] From the same text R. Johanan gave this interpretation "Hateful (to God) is the man who puts away his wife."[13]

The significant aspect of Yeshua's teaching at this point is the manner in which He grounds His understanding regarding divorce on Genesis 2:24 rather than Deuteronomy 24:1. In bringing the discussion back to the creative purpose for mankind, He once again fulfills the Torah and the Prophets by implementing what they had always taught. The oneness of husband and wife was a reflection of the oneness of God.

Marriage must be viewed as a fulfillment of God's image in man, an image that is marred by divorce. Yeshua does not invent some new teaching, nor does He initiate a new level of holiness. On the contrary, He takes us back to the very beginning—to Torah's basic teaching about the sanctity of marriage and its ability to illustrate the mystery of God's oneness.

Oaths and Vows (Matthew 5:33ff)

The misuse of vows by ancient Israel is well attested by many authorities. Outrageous vows ("May I lose my sons if ..."; "May I not see the comfort [of the Messianic age] if ...")[14] were common. This problem prompted some of the sages to make strong statements against false or hasty vows. After a typical Talmudic story of a person who swears and suffers, the sages conclude, "Be you guilty or innocent, do not swear."[15] In like manner we read:

> Be careful with vows, and not hasty with them, for he who is hasty with vows will end by false swearing, and he who swears falsely, denies me, and will never be forgiven.[16]

Since vows were taken so seriously, the legal interpretations of vows had amassed a maze of legal dicta no common person could navigate. Not unlike our current legal code, only a lawyer could decipher exactly which vows would stand and which could be circumvented. The misuse of *korban* (dedicating things to the Temple) is what prompted Yeshua's rebuke in Matthew 23, and is clearly attested in the primary sources. Thus, a system of oath-taking that had become useless for true righteousness had lost its value.

Note carefully that Yeshua prohibits swearing by things, whether by heaven or earth, Jerusalem or the altar or one's head. The matter of whether a vow was valid and binding depended, in great measure, by that to which the vow had been attached, as well as many other factors. In such a tangle of interpretation, Yeshua instructed His followers to make their vows simple and honest: "yes, yes" or "no, no."[17]

But Yeshua is not alone in such a stance. In b.*Bava Metzia* 49a, we read, "Let your nay and yea be both *zedek* (righteous)." R. Huna said, "The yea of the righteous is a yea; their no is a no."[18] According to Montefiore, "Yes, yes and no, no may be regarded as equivalent to oaths."[19] He bases this upon Rabbinic statements: R. Eleazar said, "Yea is an oath, and nay is an oath." Raba said, "But only then if yea and nay are said twice."[20] According to *Mekhilta*, the Israelites answered, "Yea, yea and nay, nay to the commands at Sinai."[21]

When Yeshua teaches "Make no vows at all," (Matthew 5:34), this must be understood in the context as a condemnation of vows made without full intent to keep them. Surely His Apostles understood His words this way. For example, James encouraged Paul to complete his Nazirite vow with four others (Acts 21:23ff). What Yeshua condemned were vows made with the "fine print" in mind that afforded loopholes so they could be broken without consequence.

As far as Torah is concerned, it is not necessary to take a vow by some object, region, or person. Nothing in the written Torah, for example, required the Nazirite vow to include a witness. Such a vow could be strictly between the individual and God. What Yeshua is calling for is a vow that is first a fervent trust between the individual and God, a vow that recognized His kingship. Only this kind of vow could ultimately gain the trust of one's fellow man and community. And only this kind of vow honors the One by whose name the vow is taken.

Eye for an Eye (Matthew 5:38ff)

Once again, Yeshua does not introduce something new, but puts what would have been considered either a light precept or one that went beyond the strict letter of the Torah on equal par with a recognized weighty law. Justice depends upon equitable retribution to the evildoer. But in a fallen world mercy and forgiveness must likewise be extended or justice becomes harsh, even cruel.

The sages clearly enjoin mercy and kindness upon the nation of Israel. "He who is yielding—who ignores a slight or a wrong—has all his sins forgiven him."[22] In another place we read:

If your fellows call you an ass, put the saddle on your shoulders.[23] As the people say, if some one says, your ears are asses' ears, give no heed; if two say it, get you a halter.[24]

Both the *Mishnah* and *Mekhilta* reject the literal interpretation of 'eye for eye' and rule that the wrongdoer has to pay damages.[25] Significant for our study, however, is the fact that in quoting Exodus 21, Yeshua begins with "eye for eye" and bypasses the opening "life for life." Clearly the rabbinic stance was to administer retaliation in kind for the taking of a life. The other measures, however, were not on the basis of retaliation but on equivalent valuation for damages rendered. While some sages favored forgiveness over retaliation, Yeshua, on the basis of His understanding of God's mercy, champions this emphasis with fervor.

It is also noteworthy that the examples Yeshua brings to His teaching do not include any form of mutilation. Smiting on the cheek is clearly an indication of personal insult, while the other two examples (suing for a coat, request for companionship on a journey) are matters of personal loss (in the first case, of a material possession, and in the second, of time; i.e., wage earning ability). Furthermore, the loss of material possessions did not require legal action, even though one could seek monetary restitution. In the request to accompany on a journey, the issue is a willingness to give up the wages these hours could have produced.

By all accounts, the whole matter of compensation for insult was in flux in the first century. Some favored heavy retaliation, while others favored forgiveness and a willingness to be defrauded.[26] Yeshua left no doubt on which side of the debate He stood. True righteousness favors forgiveness and a willingness to incur personal loss. Such willingness flows from a genuine trust in God, that He is able to meet all of one's needs. Nowhere is this demonstrated more clearly than in Yeshua's own life of obedience.

Finally

Far from abandoning the Torah, or relegating it to an inferior status, Yeshua called the people of His day, and us in our day, to embrace the Torah as God's gracious revelation of His own holiness and His instruction for our own righteous living. This Torah was given not to build men's kingdoms, but God's own kingdom of righteousness. When the Torah is unveiled to reveal the Living Torah, Yeshua, it functions as the divinely inspired foundation for the individual, the family, and the community. It is no wonder, then, that when Yeshua returns, He will establish His kingdom on the basis of Torah, for it is the eternal and unchanging revelation of the Father.

Summary

"Yeshua's Law Replaced the Law of Moses"

"The clear-cut teaching of the 'New Testament' is that the Law of Moses has been rendered inoperative with the death of Messiah; in other words, the Law in its totality no longer has authority over any individual."

Yeshua called the people of His day, and us in our day, to embrace the Torah as God's gracious revelation of His holiness and His instruction for our own righteous living. This Torah was given not to build men's kingdoms, but God's own kingdom of righteousness. When the Torah is unveiled to reveal the Living Torah, Yeshua, it functions as the divinely inspired foundation for the individual, the family, and the community.

"The Law is a unit comprised of 613 commandments, and all of it has been invalidated. No commandment has continued beyond the cross of Yeshua."

Yeshua's interpretation of the Torah was one that encouraged His listeners to return to its simple, straightforward application, one that flowed from a genuine desire to please God, not man. Far from dismissing the Torah, Yeshua was calling the people back to its holy message, one that called the people of Israel and all those who would join her into a covenant relationship with the Creator.

> **"The Law of Moses has been nullified, and we
> are now under the Law of Yeshua. The Law
> of Moses permitted vengeance—an eye for
> an eye, but the Law of Yeshua does not."**

"Both the *Mishnah* and *Mekhilta* reject the literal interpretation of 'eye for eye' and rule that the wrongdoer has to pay damages."[18] The fact that in quoting Exodus 21, Yeshua begins with "eye for eye" and bypasses the opening "life for life" shows that the rabbinic stance was to administer retaliation in kind for the taking of a life. The other measures, however, were not on the basis of retaliation but on equivalent valuation for damages rendered. While some sages favored forgiveness over retaliation, Yeshua, on the basis of His understanding of God's mercy, champions this emphasis with fervor.

Study Questions

"Yeshua's Law Replaced the Law of Moses"

1. Would the people of Yeshua's day have considered Him a prophet if He was trying to replace, or do away with, Torah? (John 4:19; 6:14; 7:40; 9:17; Deuteronomy 18:20–22)

2. How did Yeshua show that the Torah dealt with heart issues? (Matthew 5:21–26; 5:27–30)

3. What standard are we given to know if a matter is true? Isaiah 8:20

4. In Romans 10:4, "Messiah is the end of the Law" is often understood to mean the law is finished. Yet the word *end* can mean "goal": "Messiah is the goal of the Torah (Law)." In the context, which meaning fits best? (Also consider Isaiah 2:3; Malachi 4:4; Deuteronomy 29:29; Psalm 119:44.

5. Assign the following Scriptures, read aloud, and discuss: John 7:16, John 8:28, John 10:37, and John 14:8–10. Whose words did Yeshua speak? What are the implications of these verses for those who claim that Yeshua came preaching a brand-new message?

Apart from the Spirit of God,
the Torah is only letters without
life-giving power. But when the
Spirit writes the Torah upon
the heart, those same letters
reveal Yeshua, and through faith
bring life. The Spirit does not
act independently of the letter.
On the contrary, the Scriptures
are His primary tool to birth
the soul to life in Messiah.

It is Often Said

"We Have the Spirit, Who Needs the Letter?"

One afternoon, while deep in study at my desk, the phone rang. The caller inquired about our congregation—who we were, what we believed, when we met—all the standard questions. Then he asked a not-so-standard question, "Do you use commentaries when you study the Bible?" I replied that I work from the biblical texts, but that I do consult commentaries on a regular basis. The gentleman's response took me aback: "I use only the Bible because the Spirit tells me what it means, I don't need anything else." He then hastened to add, "Actually, I don't even use the Bible much anymore because the Spirit Himself tells me the truth, He speaks directly to me."

I know this is an extreme case, but hopefully it will help make my point. Today we live in an era when people try to find the truth subjectively—how they feel about what they hear or read. If they are comfortable with what they hear, or if it suits their understanding, they receive it as truth. If, on the other hand, what they hear or read is not to their liking, or in some measure upsets them or fails to give them a sense of comfort and security, it is dismissed as not true.

This subjective litmus test for truth has captivated many within the believing communities of our times. There is a greater seeking for "inner urgings" or "spiritual guidance" than there is a study of the biblical text itself based on the belief that the Spirit will subjectively guide each person. Even the obvious meaning of a given passage is fluid: It is changed and adjusted to suit one's own needs depending upon how the Spirit "leads." We hear phrases like "The Lord gave me this verse," which can sometimes be interpreted as "regardless of the clear intent of the verse, this is what it means for me."

This phenomenon is touted as proof that the present era of the "new covenant" is superior to the "old covenant."[27] We are told that whereas in ancient times they only had the "letter," now we have the "Spirit" to lead us to the truth. It's like the difference between a typewriter and a computer: Who would ever want to go back?

To support this way of thinking, verses such as 2 Corinthians 3:6 are cited: "For the letter kills, but the Spirit gives life." Was Paul teaching that a new era of the Spirit had arrived in which the sacred text of Scripture (the letter) was no longer important or at least not ultimately important? What exactly did he intend for us to understand by contrasting *letter* and *Spirit*?

Letter and Spirit in Paul

Four times in the writings of Paul, he contrasts *letter* and *Spirit*— twice in Romans and twice in 2 Corinthians. Let us look more closely at each of these as we seek to understand his meaning.

Romans 2:29

> But he is a Jew who is one inwardly; and circumci-
> sion is that which is of the heart, by the Spirit, not
> by the letter; and his praise is not from men, but
> from God.

The Context

The context of this verse is Paul's exhortation to some of the Jewish members of the Roman congregation who, apparently, were relying upon their lineage as Jews for right standing before God. Since God had made a covenant with Israel, and since the prophets described Israel as "all righteous" (Isaiah 60:21), those who were members of the covenant (and thus circumcised) considered themselves righteous in God's eyes because they were Jewish. Paul argues that being Jewish requires more than physical lineage; it involves more than circumcision of the flesh (the outward sign of the covenant). It also involves circumcision of the heart. Man looks on the outward, but God looks upon the heart. After all, the Torah speaks of being cut off from one's people,[28] a penalty for those who acted in rebellion against God and thus revealed that they were, in reality, not covenant members.

Paul surely had in mind the verses in the *Tanakh* where circumcision is defined as dealing with the heart.

> So circumcise your heart, and stiffen your neck no longer. (Deuteronomy 10:16)

> Moreover the Lord your God will circumcise your heart and the heart of your descendants, to love the LORD your God with all your heart and with all your soul, so that you may live. (Deuteronomy 30:6)

> Circumcise yourselves to the Lord and remove the foreskins of your heart, men of Judah and inhabitants of Jerusalem, or else My wrath will go forth like fire and burn with none to quench it, because of the evil of your deeds. (Jeremiah 4:4)

From these references in which the physical act of circumcision is used metaphorically to indicate a true heart of faith, the following facts may be derived. First, a circumcised heart is the opposite of rebellion (represented by the metaphor "stiff

When the Torah is written on the heart by the Spirit, a life of faith and obedience results and God's blessing—His praise—is secured.

～～

neck"). An uncircumcised heart is therefore characterized by rebellion against God. Second, a person with a circumcised heart is able to love God with one's heart and soul (living out the *Shema*—Israel's declaration of faith found in Deuteronomy 6:4–9), indicating that an uncircumcised heart is the opposite: not able to love God; that is, unable to keep His commandments. Finally, those who have uncircumcised hearts may anticipate the wrath of God's judgment, meaning they bear the penalty of their sins—they are unforgiven. An uncircumcised heart is one still weighed down with sin.

But how is the heart circumcised? There was no question how to perform physical circumcision, but how was one to circumcise the heart? The words of Ezekiel, prophesying of the time when dispersed Israel would be regathered, give us the answer.

> Then I will sprinkle clean water on you, and you will be clean; I will cleanse you from all your filthiness and from all your idols. Moreover, I will give you a new heart and put a new spirit within you; and I will remove the heart of stone from your flesh and give you a heart of flesh. I will put My Spirit within you and cause you to walk in My statutes, and you will be careful to observe My ordinances. (Ezekiel 36:25–27)

That God will "sprinkle clean water" upon the regathered exiles is a clear symbolic reference to the outpouring of the Spirit. In this spiritual regeneration, the heart of stone would be removed, and a new heart of flesh given—a circumcision of the heart. The result? Israel will walk in God's statutes and observe His ordinances. In other words, she will fulfill the *Shema*, loving God with her heart and soul, and proving her love (covenant loyalty) by obeying Him.

We should note carefully that this work of circumcising the heart is done by the Spirit. This parallels what Jeremiah promises when he writes:

> "But this is the covenant which I will make with the
> house of Israel after those days," declares the Lord,
> "I will put My Torah within them and on their heart
> I will write it; and I will be their God, and they shall
> be My people." (Jeremiah 31:34)

Here, the same "heart" language is used. The Torah, written in letters upon stone, is now also written on the heart of Israel. The result is that she walks in covenant faithfulness.

How then is Paul contrasting *letter* and *Spirit* in this verse? Speaking to Jews who believed their covenant membership was secure because of their physical lineage, Paul reminds them that a Jew who is a true covenant member is circumcised in heart as well as in flesh. A circumcised heart is one upon which the Torah is written, a "writing" that can be accomplished only by the Spirit of God. If the letters of the Torah remain upon the tablets that Moses brought down from the mountain, and are not written on the heart, they will never bring about the fulfillment of the covenant. Surely the outward rituals that they enjoin may bring the praise of men, but God looks on the heart. Only those who, by the Spirit, have the letters written on the heart (meaning their lives are governed by those letters of Torah) will receive the blessings of the covenant, and may therefore rightly be called covenant members.

Paul is not contrasting *letter* and *Spirit* as though one is bad and the other good. On the contrary, he is teaching that the letter, apart from the work of the Spirit, cannot bring the blessings of the covenant. The letter (the covenant) must be written on the heart (a work only the Spirit can do) in order for true covenant membership to be enjoyed. When the Torah is written on the heart by the Spirit, a life of faith and obedience results and God's blessing—His praise—is secured.

Romans 7:6

> But now we have been released from the Torah, having died to that by which we were bound, so that we serve in newness of the Spirit and not in oldness of the letter.

The Context

Paul has used the analogy of a marriage covenant. As long as both husband and wife are living, they are bound to each other by the stipulations of that covenant. If the husband dies, however, the stipulations of the marriage covenant that bind the wife to her husband are over and she is free to remarry.

But Paul is not giving us a treatise on the law of marriage. He is using the marriage covenant as a fitting illustration of his central point: Legal jurisdiction is broken when a person dies. The stipulations of the marriage covenant can no longer be enforced when one member of the marriage is no longer living.

It is important to understand how this analogy fits Paul's main point in this passage. He has already taught that the believer in Yeshua has died with Him and risen to a new life (6:3–7). The believer has died vicariously—Yeshua has died in his place, and the Father counts Yeshua's death as though the sinner had actually died. Before the believer died with Messiah, however, the penalty of the Torah was binding upon him: "The soul who sins will die" (Ezekiel 18:4). But once the believer has died with Messiah, the condemnation of the Torah that once bound him is done away with. Even as the wife is free from the marriage covenant once her husband passes away, so the believer is released from the penalty for sin prescribed by the Torah since he has died with Messiah. Death has severed the Torah's ability to condemn.

It is important to understand that it is not the Torah that died—it is the sinner who died in Messiah. Paul makes it clear that there is nothing wrong with the Torah.

> What shall we say then? Is the Torah sin? May it never be! On the contrary, I would not have come to know sin except through the Torah. (Romans 7:7)

Thus, having died in Messiah, the one who was bound (married, in the metaphor) to sin is now free to be joined to another, that is, to Messiah (7:4, cf. 6:22). The condemnation of the Torah, which is prescribed as the wages of sin, can no longer be administered. The one who is joined to the Messiah need never again fear that God's justice, administered through the Torah, would condemn him.

It is in this line of thinking that Paul brings up the contrast of the letter and the Spirit. As long as the Torah functioned only as a law code without the ability to change the heart (change one's unrighteous behavior), the Torah could only condemn—it could never bring life. But once the heart is changed from stone to a heart of flesh—once the Spirit writes the Torah upon the heart—then the "obedience of faith"[29] becomes the life of the believer. Thus, the "oldness of the letter" is Paul's characterization of life lived apart from the inward work of the Spirit writing the Torah upon the heart. The "old letter" is the Torah without the Spirit.

On the other hand, the "newness of the Spirit" speaks of the newness of the Torah as it is written upon the heart by the Spirit. Paul knew this firsthand. In 7:9 he writes:

> I was once alive apart from the Torah; but when the commandment came, sin became alive and I died;

We might rightly ask, "When was Paul alive 'apart from the Torah'?" All of his life was engulfed in the Torah, from his youth. How could Paul say that he was once "alive apart from the Torah"? Not only this, but he confesses that the "commandment came," meaning there was a time in his life when the commandment had not yet come. Is this possible for the "Pharisee of Pharisees"? The answer, of course, is yes! But what does this mean? Its meaning must be that there was a time in Paul's life when the Torah was only "letter" without the work of the Spirit. It was there, written on parchment with ink in all its beauty.

But it was only letters on parchment—it had not changed the heart of Saul. But when God, in His sovereign power, placed His love upon Paul, He wrote on his heart that very same Torah that Paul had read from letters on parchment, and then the Torah began its life-changing work—"the commandment came."

Up until that time, Paul was "alive"—nothing was amiss. He was praised by men as one of the most zealous for the Torah. He thought of himself in this way: "as to the righteousness which is in the Torah, found blameless" (Philippians 3:6). Everything was good—Paul was alive! But when the Spirit wrote the Torah on his heart, his sin became fully known, and Paul died. He died to self and to sin. This life-changing work of the Torah could not happen when it remained as letters on parchment—it had to be written on the heart by the Spirit.

Thus, the "newness of the Spirit" refers to the new work of the Torah when written on the heart by the Spirit. And the "oldness of the letter" is Torah apart from the Spirit, unable to effect true righteousness in the life of a sinner.

2 Corinthians 3:6 and 3:15–17

Who also made us adequate as servants of a new covenant, not of the letter but of the Spirit; for the letter kills, but the Spirit gives life.

When left as letters without the life-giving work of the Spirit, the Gospel in the Torah that points to Yeshua is veiled. Only the Spirit can remove the veil by writing the Torah on the heart.

The Context

Paul was facing a challenge of his credentials as he wrote to the Corinthian congregation. Apparently there were those who disagreed with Paul's teaching and were suggesting that he did not have the proper credentials (perhaps proper rabbinic ordination?) to be instructing the Torah community of Corinth. Paul countered by claiming the Corinthians themselves as his credentials. He was not depending upon letters written with ink, but on the changed lives of the Corinthians—a change that came as a result of their receiving the gospel that Paul had preached. The Torah had been written on their hearts by the Spirit of God, and this resulted in a genuine change of life. This evident change was proof that the Gospel message given by Paul and received by the Corinthians was authentic, for it had been used by God to bring about righteousness in their lives.

Those who were opposing Paul, however, were preaching a different gospel. What exactly they were teaching is not certain, but one can imagine that they were claiming covenant membership on the basis of Jewish lineage, and therefore the Gentiles needed to undergo the ceremony of a proselyte (i.e., "become a Jew") in order to enter the covenant. They were teaching that Moses was enough; Paul was saying that Moses pointed to the Messiah.

It is in this context that Paul parallels his ministry with that of Moses. Everyone would agree that Moses had impeccable credentials: He was chosen by God and he received the very

Torah, written by the finger of God. How could anyone even think Paul's ministry could be compared to that of Moses?

Paul's criteria for the comparison were the people affected by the ministry of each. How obedient to God were the people whom Moses led? Did their lives change for righteousness the way the lives of the Corinthians had changed? When put that way, the effect of Paul's ministry was superior, for Israel was characterized by her rebellion under the leadership of Moses— of all the adult men who crossed the Red Sea during God's great redemption from Egypt, only Joshua and Caleb made it into the Promised Land.

So what made the difference? Both Paul and Moses were divinely called to their ministry. And both preached the same message—the Gospel that pointed to faith in the Messiah.[30] Why then was Paul's ministry effective in bringing people to faith while Moses' ministry was not (at least when one considers the actions of Israel as a whole)?

The difference, from Paul's perspective, was the presence of a veil. When Moses came down from the mountain, he had been face to face with Yeshua. Exodus 24:10 makes it clear that Moses, Aaron, and the elders who were with them "saw the God of Israel." The visible manifestation of God, from Paul's point of view, is always connected to the Messiah. So when Moses entered the cloud, he spoke face to face with the Son of God. It was therefore Yeshua's glory that was shining in his face as he descended the mountain, and it was Yeshua's glory that was veiled so that the people would not see it.[31] And since Paul can use "Moses" to refer to the Torah ("But to this day whenever Moses is read ..." 2 Corinthians 3:15), he can also reason that the Torah is veiled. Though one should see the glory of Yeshua in the Torah, when it is veiled, Yeshua is hidden.

This same veil also lies over the hearts of those who do not find Yeshua in the Torah:

But to this day whenever Moses is read, a veil lies over their heart; but whenever a person turns to the Lord, the veil is taken away. (vv. 15–16)

The veil is the absence of the Spirit's work in connection with the Scriptures. When the Spirit brings the Scriptures alive by writing them on the heart, Yeshua is no longer veiled in those Scriptures—He is plainly seen.

Once again, the issue is a matter of the heart. When the Torah remains as letters on stone or parchment, it has no power to affect righteousness. When left as letters without the life-giving work of the Spirit, the Gospel in the Torah that points to Yeshua is veiled.[32] Only the Spirit can remove the veil by writing the Torah on the heart.

Surely Paul is not diminishing the inspired words of His Bible, the Torah! When the veil is taken away, and Moses is read through the work of the Spirit writing it on the heart, then Yeshua is not only seen, but also embraced by faith. And the same letters engraved on stone are the letters written on the heart by the Spirit.

Paul is consistent with his use of *letter* and *Spirit*. Here, as in Romans, the letters on stones or parchment accomplish their mission of condemnation. They condemn the sinner. Only when the letters of the eternal Torah are written on the heart—when the veil is taken away from Moses by the sovereign work of the Spirit—only then does the glory of Yeshua shine forth in the letters of the Torah. And when this glory is seen through eyes of faith, eternal life is the inevitable result.

Finally

The contrast between *letter* and *Spirit* used by Paul in Romans and 2 Corinthians does not set at odds the eternal Word of God (the Torah) and the work of the Spirit. Far from it! When the contexts are studied, and the words of Paul are given their intended meaning, the contrast Paul wishes to emphasize is the Word of God (Torah) without the Spirit and the Word of God with the Spirit. Apart from the Spirit of God, the Torah is only letters without life-giving power. In fact, apart from the Spirit's work, the words of Torah condemn the sinner. But when the Spirit writes the Torah upon the heart, those same letters reveal Yeshua, and through faith bring life. The Spirit does not act independently of the letter. On the contrary, the Scriptures are His primary tool to birth the soul to life in Messiah.

Summary

"We Have the Spirit, Who Needs the Letter?"

"Members of the body of Messiah are dead to the Law; the Law could not justify, bring righteousness or life; in fact, because of the Law, its followers were dead spiritually!"

The letter, apart from the work of the Spirit (apart from faith), cannot bring the blessings of the covenant (justification, righteousness, and life); there is only condemnation and death. The letter (the covenant) must be written on the heart (a work only the Spirit can do, through faith) in order for true covenant membership to be enjoyed. When the Torah is written on the heart by the Spirit, a life of faith and obedience results and God's blessing—His praise—is secured.

"Not only was the Law abrogated when Messiah came, we are also dead to Law. Thus, not only are we not justified by keeping it, we are not to subject ourselves to it. To do so is to be disloyal to Messiah."

It is important to understand that it is not the Torah that died—it is the sinner who died in Messiah. Paul makes it clear that there is nothing wrong with the Torah (Romans 7:7). Thus, having died in the Messiah, the one who was "bound" to sin is now free to be joined to another; that is, to Messiah (Romans 7:4; cf. 6:22). The condemnation of the Torah, which is prescribed as the wages of sin, can no longer be administered. The one who is joined to Messiah need never again fear that God's justice, administered through the Torah, would condemn him.

> **"Because we are serving God in the newness of the Spirit and not in the oldness of the Letter, we are free to choose which laws in the 'Old Testament' we want to keep."**

To say that we serve God in the "newness of the Spirit" means that the Torah is written on our hearts, not only on pieces of stone or parchment in the "oldness of the letter." Since the Torah is now written on the heart it reveals the Gospel that points to Yeshua, thus giving it power to affect righteousness. The "newness of the Spirit" does not diminish the inspired words of Torah, but brings them alive and exalts them with the revelation of Yeshua as the ultimate goal of righteousness.

Study Questions

"We Have the Spirit, Who Needs the Letter?"

1. In reference to Romans 2:29, what is physical circumcision supposed to represent? (Genesis 15:5–6; 17:4–11)

2. How was the spiritual lesson of physical circumcision revealed in ancient Israel? Can it be found in the Torah?

3. Those who consider that the Torah has been abolished often do so because they consider the Torah (Law) to be bad. Consider Romans 7:7ff in light of this idea. What conclusion did Paul reach regarding the value of the Torah?

4. Before we knew God, to what were we bound: righteousness or sin? (Romans 6:6–7; 1 John 3:5) What is sin? (1 John 3:4) Now that we are free from the penalty of sin, what are we to do? (Romans 8:7–9; 2 Timothy 2:22)

5. How does the Spirit use the Torah to accomplish holiness in the lives of believers? How does this relate to Paul's use of the phrase "the newness of the Spirit"? (Romans 7:6)

6. According to Paul, what does the Torah do if not accompanied by the work of the Spirit? (2 Corinthians 3:6)

7. How are the Scriptures used by the Spirit in His ongoing work of sanctification in the life a believer? Did the Spirit work this same way before the coming of Yeshua, and if so, how?

Endnotes

[1] Ephraim Urbach, *The Sages* (Harvard, 1979), 345.

[2] b.*Shevuot* 12b.

[3] Sifre *Deuteronomy* §76.

[4] Urbach, *The Sages* (Harvard Univ. Press, 1979), 346.

[5] The Greek text of Matthew 5:18 speaks of the "least" commandment, but the common Hebrew terms are a "light commandment" and a "weighty commandment."

[6] m.*Avot* 2.1.

[7] Sifre *Deuteronomy* 22:13. quoted from David Flusser, "The Sermon on the Mount" in *Judaism and the Origins of Christianity* (Magnes Press, 1988), 501. Cf. also t.*Sotah* 5:11, cp. b.*Kiddushin* 41a. Note also the many references Flusser lists as pertaining to hatred leading to and thus equal to murder in Op. cit., 501 n. 34 and his comments on 502-3.

[8] C. G. Montefiore, *Rabbinic Literature and Gospel Teachings* (KTAV, 1970), 41.

[9] *Mekhilta* R. Simeon p. iii, quoted from Montefiore, Ibid.

[10] In Mid. Rab. *Leviticus* xxiii.12 on Ex 18:3).

[11] b.*Yoma* 29a. See the many examples given in J. Foote Moore, *Judaism* 3 vols (Hendrickson, 1997), 2.267ff.

[12] b.*Gittin* 90b.

[13] Ibid.

[14] b.*Shabbat* 116a; b.*Bava Metzia* 85a; b. *Makkot* 5b

[15] y.*Shevuot* vi. §6, 37a. Quoted from Montefiore, Op. cit., 49.

[16] Tanchuma *Bereishit* 1.1; b.*Mattot* 79a.

[17] Matthew 5:37.

[18] Mid. Rab. *Ruth* vii. §6, on 3.18.

[19] Montefiore, Op. cit., 49.

[20] b.*Shavuot* 36a.

[21] *Mekhilta* on Exodus 20:1,2.

[22] b.*Yoma* 23a.

[23] b.*Bava Kamma* 92a.

24 Mid. Rab. *Genesis* xlv. 7 on Gen 16:9.

25 David Daube, *The New Testament and Rabbinic Judaism* (London: School of Oriental and African Studies, 1956), 255.

26 Daube, Ibid., 263-64.

27 These are the way the terms "new covenant" and "old covenant" are often used, to mean "God's Word back then" as opposed to "God's Word now." However, this is not what the terms mean.

28 Genesis 17:14; Exodus 30:33, 38; 31:14; Leviticus 7:20, 25, 27; 17:4, 9; 18:29; 19:8; 20:5, 17; 23:29; Numbers 9:13; 15:30.

29 Romans 1:5; 16:26; cf. 15:8.

30 Note Romans 10:8ff, where Paul quotes Deuteronomy 30:14ff and labels these words of Moses as "the word of faith which we are preaching."

31 The English translations that indicate that the glory in Moses' face was "fading" are amiss. The Greek verb, *katargeo*, translated "fading" or "fading away," does not actually have this meaning. *Katargeo* means "to render ineffective," "to abolish," or "to destroy" (cf. *BDAG*, 525). The veil was put over Moses' face, not because the glory was fading, but in order to render the glory ineffective. The glory in Moses' face, as far as Paul is concerned, would have led the people to know the One whose glory it was. But the veil made this impossible. For further explanation of 2 Corinthians 3 and the veil over Moses' face, see "What's So New about the New Covenant?" available from www.ffoz. org.

32 2 Corinthians 4:3.